Mohamed is a full-time assurance and advisory consultant, he has worked in Oil & Gas, Finance and Real Estate. Leveraging his expertise in the field and learning experience, he created a practical guide for effective consulting engagements.

Mohamed AlNuaimi

CONSULTANT STRATEGIES FOR NEW PROFESSIONALS IN THE FIELD

AUSTIN MACAULEY PUBLISHERS™

LONDON · CAMBRIDGE · NEW YORK · SHARJAH

The age group that matches the content of the books has been classified according to the age classification system issued by the Ministry of Culture and Youth.

ISBN – 9789948779841 – (Paperback)
ISBN – 9789948779858 – (E-Book)

Application Number: MC-10-01-7917580
Age Classification: E

Printer Name: iPrint Global Ltd
Printer Address: Witchford, England

First Published 2023
AUSTIN MACAULEY PUBLISHERS FZE
Sharjah Publishing City
P.O Box [519201]
Sharjah, UAE
www.austinmacauley.ae
+971 655 95 202

Table of Content

Module 1: Introduction

When you're a new consultant, getting started might sound difficult, daunting, and even downright challenging. Well, the fact of the matter is that getting started is always the hardest part of doing anything. But not worry – this eBook is specifically designed to help you learn the right strategies to get started in the field. From basic consultant strategies to learning how to engage with clients to taking on new projects and building a team from the ground up, you'll learn about it all in this eBook.

If you're ready to get started, let's begin with the first chapter. Here, we'll talk about one of the fundamental aspects of starting your very own consulting business – connecting with a client and analyzing their business.

Learning Outcomes

At the end of this chapter, students are expected to have understood:

- Detailed characteristics of a company profile
- Method to devise a business plan summary
- Various types of process objectives

Client Analysis

When you first take on a new client, it's important to get to know their business on a deeper level. As a consultant, your role is to essentially provide clients with services that they cannot do themselves. This is likely why they've contacted you, to begin with. During the client analysis stage, you're going to take the time to connect with your client personally.

We always recommend presenting yourself as an extension of their business. In this way, you can provide them with tailored and personalized support that truly meets their needs and exceeds their expectations. Your goal is to handle their pain points so that they can focus on what's most important for them – running their business.

You can begin your client analysis with a thoughtful information collection process that allows you to build a company profile. Your company profile should include a list of critical details about your client. This information will allow you to get to know their business better on a fundamental level, while also giving you the insight that you need to further tailor their experience working with you. Take a look at the information down below to get a better idea of just what a company profile is and what it should include.

Company Profile

A company profile is a summarized version of a business and its operations. It is devised for professional use. Company profile is majorly generated to raise funds, attract investors, and keep the stakeholders in the loop. This provides clear information that the clients need to know and have the information of. A company profile is meant to introduce your products or services to the target audience and future investors.

Let's have a look at the components of a basic company profile.

Introduction of the Company

This includes the name of the company, the official website of the company, the physical location, date of establishment, and all the other contact information. In this section, you can also add a brief history of your company and details that might be important to highlight.

Vision, Mission, Strategy

The vision highlights the future goals of a company. It talks about where the company wants to be and its future position. A mission statement includes the objectives of the company. Strategy is the approach to achieve these objectives and be at the predicted future position.

Organizational Structure

As the term suggests, it is the structure of the organization. The structure of activities in the organization and how the chain of command works in the company. This can include the roles and responsibilities of the employees. Moreover, the rules and ethics to conduct these activities in a professional environment.

Key Person's Profile

The key person can be the CEO or the owner of the company. Brief information about this person is also included in the company's profile as the people need to know who has the decision-making power and complete hold of the company.

Nature of Products and Services

Adding the nature of products and services is essential in a company profile. As this profile is primarily for buyers and stakeholders, they need to know what kind of products you are selling or services you are offering. This information is vital to sell and market your product or services.

Existing Clients or Core Business Areas that You Are Targeting Your Business

Details of existing clients are important to keep a track of your clients and their records. A company can determine where they stand in terms of clients. A list of business areas is also included in this profile to devise a proper plan.

Details of Projects Undertaken or Capable of Handling

Upcoming or existing projects are mentioned in the profile to record the position of the company and the workload of the company. This helps the company to measure its resources and abilities to complete and take up more projects.

Work Exception Flow Chart

This gives an idea of the workflow of the company. Working practices and ethics followed by the company are also a part of this section. Various processes are separated through steps of work. This can include manufacturing processes or packaging, etc.

Details of Key Persons to Be Contacted

This is a list of contact information of the key persons of the company. The people who are directly impacted by the company and who hold great responsibility. These people are the ones who are contacted in the case of any sort of emergency.

Accreditations and Recognitions

This section includes any sort of certification of recognition that the company has received. For example, national recognition for producing biodegradable packaging of your product. These can be given by national or international bodies.

Once you've built a comprehensive company profile, all you have is a clear document that gives you fundamental information related to your client. Next, you'll want to dive a bit deeper.

Detailed Profile

In this next process, you'll conduct a more detailed profile analysis. Here, you'll look for new details around a critical set of criteria to help you gain a more comprehensive understanding of your client's processes, operations, and pain points.

Management

This talks about the overall management of the company; Who owns what percentage of the company, what is the hierarchy for decision-making. The important managerial position holders, the entire team in a business or all the employees of the company come under this section. Important ones are highlighted in this section.

Products and Services

You need to dig deeper into the products and services provided by the company: the types of products and services: are they tangible or intangible? Do they count as intellectual property? If yes, then how to register for them and protect them? The resources allocated and further required to make these products and deliver these services.

Target Market, Competition and Marketing Strategies

Target audience is very important in this; as for marketing strategies, the company needs to know their consumers. A list of competitors helps the company to know about their competition better and bring innovation in the services they offer. Companies can also define a USP by analyzing the competitors.

Budget, Source and Nature of Funding

Budget is essential as it is the backbone of the entire company. An allocated budget in a company profile helps the stakeholders have a better idea about the expansion, resources, and ability of the company to thrive. The source of funding gives a clearer idea of where the money is coming from and how consistent it is.

Infrastructure Requirements and Cost

Infrastructure requirement helps the company allocated enough money in the budget for infrastructure that it can sustain and bear the costs. The costs are determined at the start which helps the project to move smoothly.

Plan Implementation

As mentioned earlier, there are set missions and visions of a company. They help the company devise a plan. The implementation to gct this plan in aclion is also mentioned in the company profile so that a clearer idea of the way forward is given.

Staff Salaries and Incentives

Workers are essential in any and every company. Without them, it's almost impossible to keep the company going. Their salaries and incentives are mentioned in the business profile to allocate a specific budget to them.

Pricing

Pricing is vital because this shows the revenue you would generate keeping the profit in mind. Any pricing strategy can be adopted by the company. Businesses can look at its growth and decide the kind of pricing they think is suitable.

Income and Expenditure

Income and expenditure are very important for a company. The revenue earned needs to be studied properly and the division of future expenditure and profit should be done accordingly. These things are listed in a profile because this shows the size of the company and its production line. This gives a clearer idea of how much a company earns and spends.

Repayment

Knowing your expenses is good and knowing how much you owe someone is even more important. Keeping a list of repayments in your company profile shows how responsible you are. This gives a clearer idea to the stakeholders regarding your position.

Cash Flow, Breakeven and Profitability Statements

As mentioned above, the financial condition of the company is extremely vital to the stakeholders. Giving them all the information regarding cash flow, break-even, and profitability statements helps them look at the business' position in the market and how the business is doing overall.

Risk Factors

Risk factors need to be written in detail for the stakeholders to know what they are getting into. The buyers also need to be aware of things or situations that can cause hindrance in the future. This helps everyone directly impacted by the company to be prepared to deal with any problem that arises in the future.

Once you've determined your clients' processes, operations, and pain points, it'll be time to get to the root of what you do as a consultant. Here, you'll begin to develop the framework within which you'll situate your services. You'll have to build a team – or if you choose to go it alone, you'll want to fill your client's team's in on what you plan to do. Begin with the problem that you're looking to solve, and then show them just what you plan to do to solve it.

Prove to them what it is that makes your services unique when compared to other consultants. This is your chance to shine and showcase just what you're capable of. Take a look at some quick facts below to help you with this stage of the process.

Quick Facts

- Team: Describe the persons behind the project and their role succinctly. This motivates your workforce that they are being acknowledged.
- Problem: What problem are you attempting to solve? Is it even a problem? Look deeply into the issue you are facing as it might be something that can be sorted out easily.

- Advantages: What makes your service unique? What distinguishes you from others? Analyze how you have an advantage over others and what edge you have?

- Solution: Describe how you intend to address the issue. Give a clearer view of your solution. This will help everyone understand and everyone can work on the implementation of the solution.

- Product: How does your product or service function? Give a few examples. Give a demonstration of your product or service. Everyone needs to understand what the product or service is like.

- Traction: Traction is the collection of quantifiable customers that serve to demonstrate a product's potential. This is important because if traction is lacking then it will negatively impact your customer base and dry up your sales.

- Market: Determine or at least make an attempt to estimate the size of your target market. Having knowledge about your market and its analysis is very important. This helps you efficiently market your product.

- Competition: What are the alternate solutions to the issue you're attempting to solve? Look at the competitors, study them and analyze their products. This helps you define your unique selling point and your marketing techniques.

- Business Model: How do you intend to generate revenue? Show a schedule when you expect revenues to pour in. A business model highlights a company's plan for making profits. This can help you predict cash inflow.

- Investing: What is your projected budget for investments? What type of cash are you seeking? The resources required for your project are important and you should have all the details about that. This helps to have enough capital available to finish your project and keep track.
- Contact: Include your contact information and make it easy for folks to reach you. Don't make people wait or struggle to contact you. Don't make contacting you too complicated. Leave out your details for the people interested.

Remember, you need to make yourself stand out from other consultants in your field. You can do this by leveraging a few built-in competitive advantages that you can embrace from the moment you start marketing yourself as a consultant. Take a look down below to learn more about the steps you can take to showcase your abilities.

Competitive Advantages

These are the factors that permit a company to produce goods and services at a cheaper rate or in a better way to stand out in the market and get an advantage over your rival. The company would outperform its competitors and generate more sales hence more revenue.

Proposition of Customer Value

Any strategy statement that fails to demonstrate why customers should purchase the products or services is bound to fail. A simple visual that compares your value proposition to that of your competitors can be a highly efficient and straightforward method for discovering what makes you unique.

Differentiation Elements

Recognizing the unique operations or complicated set of activities that enable the company to provide its value proposition to customers on its own.

Once your client has chosen to work with you, you need to help them develop some clear and effective business goals that highlight the strategy you've put in place, the solution you plan to offer, and the vision that your client sees for their business after enlisting your services and support.

We always recommend drafting out a set of business goals to make sure that everyone involved is on the same page. Take a look down below to learn more about what these business goals should entail.

Business Goals

These are set objectives of aims that a business wants to achieve in a set period. Goals and objectives are something that keeps the employees motivated to work hard and accomplish. These are the outcomes that the company wants to achieve in the longer run. Business goals can be short-term as well as long-term. These goals help the company to measure its success and ensure that the company is on the right path.

Executive Summary

These are some pointers that need to be considered when setting or examining business goals.

What is the business? The type of business would be mentioned and the kind of operations that will take place in this. This should be mentioned but concisely.

Set goals under achievable parameters and time specifics. Your goals should be SMART. This implies that your objectives must be specific, quantifiable, attainable, pertinent, and time bound.

Provide provision for re-setting the goals, if needed. You should always have room for improvement or change. You might have to change your objectives and goals in the middle, so you should always have this window of resetting them.

Daily, weekly, or monthly, list your short and long-term objectives. This helps you get motivated and be consistent with work so that you can achieve all sorts of goals and objectives.

Investment Guide

Develop a business plan with a defined vision, mission, and strategy. Develop an objective, a single precise driver of business for several years (specific, measurable & time-bound). Make an actionable strategic statement. Define scale of investment. Identify the sector. Analyze present market conditions. Visualize future prospects and risks. Prepare exit measures. Consult experts to keep a watch to avert any unfortunate situations.

Business Plan Summary

A business plan summary is a brief explanation and introduction of your entire plan of running your business. This describes the type of business you have, the unique selling point, the solution your product or service provides, target market, financial requirements, and other risk factors. This summary shortens a long business report for a quick understanding of the business.

The purpose of constructing a business plan summary is that it creates a functional and effective strategy for growth which gives a way forward to the business. This summary also helps your company to determine and predict your future financial requirements and needs. You can identify your future expenses and make a budget out of this summary. Lastly, a business plan summary is used to attract investors for business expansion and funding.

Business setup

This talks about the type of organization. There are many structures of business, and you can adopt any according to your requirement. The type of setup includes sole ownership, partnership, corporation, or limited liability company.

Product/Service

In this section, a brief description of your company's products and services is given. All the products or services offered by the business are mentioned. This section also includes the details such as the market differentials, competitive advantage, and unique selling point of the services you provide.

Market

An overview of the market is provided here. The kind of market the business deals in and an analysis is presented. The industry that your company is involved in, the competitors in this market. How these competitors sustain in the market and what is the potential of this market. The target audience is also mentioned in detail in this section.

Marketing Plan

This highlights the strategy that the business needs to adopt to advertise its product or service. Complete market research is conducted and by considering all the findings, a strategy and plan are devised to launch this product in the market and boost sales.

4 Ps

A complete marketing plan requires a perfect combination of all four marketing Ps. These are Place, Product, Promotion, and Price. Product is the kind of item that you sell that can be tangible or intangible. Price is the amount that you charge for the goods you sell. This price is set after the market and competitor analysis. The place is the platform where you promote your product. What is the source or place your customers get the information from? Promotion is how you effectively showcase your product and how you reach your customers.

Employment

Employment will cover the number of employees a company requires and the kind of employment contracts they need. The number of employees is also a factor that measures the size of the company. Moreover, the company might require 60% employees on a full-time basis, 30% on a part-time basis, and 10% on a contract basis. This is also defined in a business plan.

Financial Forecast

The business's future outcomes are estimated and predicted with the help of previous records. Projected growth income analysis is performed to see how much the business will grow in the future and the money that will be generated. Break-even analysis is also a part of this forecast as this analysis gives us an idea of how many units should be sold to cover the manufacturing cost.

Financial Requirements

This is regarding the essential money required for all the operations to be carried out in a business. This section should have a detailed statement of the capital that is required for the business to work. Finances are required on an emergency basis or if there is an expansion planned in the future. All the financial requirements are noted down and presented in a business plan.

Sensitivity/Risk Analysis

The risks a company might face in the future or how sensitive it is to changes in the market are analyzed in this section and presented in the plan so that everyone is aware. Moreover, the company can prepare itself to deal with these issues if they encounter them.

Process Objectives

These are the ultimate goals and targeted destination points that management wants to achieve through a series of actions, procedures, documentation, and decisions carried out by employees.

They cover the following dimensions:

- Operational

These are the objectives that are essential in collaborating and incorporating management and operations into the planning process. This helps to achieve the strategic goals of the company.

- Technological

This can be related to the technology being used or needed by the business to carry out its goals to have better machinery or updated software for business.

- Financial

These are basically the future financial needs and goals of a business. The exact amount they are predicting to earn or a certain profit they want to achieve falls under financial objectives.

- Environmental

The business has a responsibility to be environment-friendly and every company has specific objectives to improve its environmental performance. This is done by decreasing the number of harmful emissions etc.

- Strategic

These objectives can be some sort of performance goal. It's the approach of the company to achieve its mission and vision. These goals are linked to the implementation of strategies.

- Social

Social objectives are closely linked with the well-being of society and individuals. These objectives include good quality of goods and services, reasonable prices, and contribution to social welfare and the betterment of society.

Ways to obtain understanding (gradually getting into the process within the scope). The process flow can be obtained by several means:

1. Workshop with the key personnel
2. One-on-one interviews (Question on a separate paper – evidence – conclusion)

3. Observations

To further understand the processes, break them down into:

1. Inputs (documents, sub-processes, data, etc.)
2. Activities involving processing of inputs
3. Outputs

Ask Yourself

1. What processes and sub-processes need to be covered as per scope?
2. Who are the process owners?
3. Who performs an activity?
4. How is the activity performed? (System/Manual)
5. When is the activity performed? (frequency/intervals)
6. Where is the activity performed?

End of Module Questions

1. Which of the following is not a major function of a company profile?
   a) To summarize your products and services
   b) To attract and retain investors
   c) To maintain a strong social media presence
   d) To keep stakeholders informed
2. Which of the following elements is considered the backbone of a company?

a) Budget

b) Market

c) Investors

d) Stakeholders

3. Why do you need to describe and be aware of your risk factors?

   a) To showcase the current and potential hindrances

   b) To know the solvency of your company

   c) To decrease the liabilities on your company

   d) To make a better case for your market

4. If you can produce goods at a cost lower than that of your competitors, you are most likely to have:

   a) Better resources

   b) A competitive advantage

   c) A better market

   d) More employees

5. Which of the following two are the most important characteristics for your business objective to have?

   i. Measurability

   ii. Timing

   iii. Specificity

   iv. Actionability

a) ii and iv

b) iii and iv

c) i and iii

d) ii and iii

6. Which of the following is not one of the four Ps of a complete marketing plan?

   a) People

   b) Product

   c) Place

d) Promotion

7. Which section of the business plan summary should a detailed statement of the necessary business capital be included in?
   a) Financial forecast
   b) Marketing plan
   c) Financial requirements
   d) Business setup

8. Fill in the blank.

The __________ dimension of process objectives deals with the approach of the company to achieve its mission.
   a) Operational
   b) Social
   c) Strategic
   d) None of the above

Module 2: Documenting the Process Flow

Process flow gives an overview of the entire workflow. It involves all the tasks, objectives, goals, and deadlines. All the possible outcomes of any problem or risks are mentioned in this flow so that everyone is prepared for any sort of issue in the future. This flow also shows relationships between different components of a process.

- Processes/Process Inputs
- Process Outputs
- Control Points
- IT Applications impacting the process
- System Narratives

Learning Outcomes

At the end of this chapter, students are expected to have understood:

- Features of a process flow
- Importance of controls

- Identification of risks
- Usage and importance of data sources

Process

1. Objectives

What is the entity / department / function / business trying to do? The goals of starting the entire process should be defined and clear to the entire team.

2. Risks

What are the potential events that could affect the achievement of the objectives? What could go wrong? Predict all sorts of risks and mishaps that can take place and be prepared to counter them during the process.

3. Controls

What are the actions the department should take to mitigate the risks? After analyzing the risks that might be encountered, your company should find solutions that can resolve potential risks.

4. Alignment

Between risk, objectives, and controls, a process requires a concrete structure which means you need to maintain an alignment between the objectives, risks, and controls you have in this process.

Sources of Process, Objectives, and Risks

1. Strategic or Operational Plans

A strategic plan is a plan devised by the company to accomplish its long-term goals. It is the approach used to achieve the vision drafted by the company whereas operational plans are things that need to be done to attain the company's strategic plan. Objectives of the company are achieved through operational plans.

Several types of strategic plans are:

- Corporate: A corporate strategy plan to develop ten products can be devised to achieve an overall increase in revenue. In this case, developing products is a strategic plan whereas increasing revenue is the goal.
- Marketing: To boost and accomplish a gross margin of 38%, a plan is constructed of using digital platforms for the advertising and promotion of your product. In this case, the goal or the vision is to achieve a 38% gross margin and the strategic marketing plan is the promotion of products on digital platforms.

Some examples of operational plans are:

- Contingency Operational Plans
- Processes & Practices Operational Plans
- Go-to-market Operational Plans

- Minutes of Board Meetings

These are the decisions and actions taken by the board members in a meeting. These are the official record of these important meetings in which detailed and important discussions are held. Critical decisions are stated in these minutes of board meetings. Some important features of minutes are listed below:

- Written in clear and coherent language and structure
- Maintain minutes book
- Should be brief and to the point
- Preferably written by hand

- Workshops with Process Owners

Process owners are the individuals who are directly responsible for generating, sustaining, and improving a specific process. They are accountable for the outcomes of the process too. The workshops given to them can help work efficiently and reflect improvement in the process they are carrying out.

There are many benefits of attending workshops and some of them are listed below.

- Innovative ways of thinking
- Inspiration to work effectively
- Learn new skills
- More opportunities for expanding professional network

- Internal Reports

These are the reports that have a compilation of financial operational information of your business. These reports are distributed within the company so that the performance can be improved. These reports are not for the outsiders, they remain within the company.

> Types of Internal Reports
>   - Routine Reports: These reports are basic and general. They are submitted before the management on a weekly, monthly, or quarterly basis. These reports can be related to sales, production costs, funds or schedules, and deadlines.
>   - Special Reports: These reports are prepared on-demand. These reports are especially demanded by the management on a specific matter. This doesn't include routine information. This can include cost reduction schemes, the impact of a labor dispute, or the introduction of new products.
>   - Management Level Reports: These are level-specific reports and are not useful for all the employees of the company. The report for lower-level staff will be different from the report for the top managerial level. Reports can be for the general manager, foreman, board of directors, or the company secretary.

- Laws and Regulations

These are the rules and regulations that should be followed by anyone professionally associated with the company or who works there. These laws are drafted to protect the business and the employees. Some of the laws and regulations that should be followed are:

- Confidentiality
- Protection of Human Resources
- Environmental Protection
- Fair Competition

- Customer Complaints

Customer complaints are the reservations expressed by the customers if there is a gap between the promise made by the business and the product or service delivered. If the company is unable to deliver what was expected from them, then the customers file complaints with the business. Several examples of customer complaints are:

- Poor product or service
- No follow up
- Repetitive customer problem

Risks and Controls

Objectives, Risks and Control Matrix

This matrix is a powerful tool that can help your company to analyze and identify your risks. Furthermore, this tool also implements the control which eliminates the risks and puts your process back on track. Once this is done, the process is back to achieving objectives set at the start of the process.

The questions answered by this matrix are the following:

- What (existing control)?
- Who Performs?
- When (frequency)?
- How – preventive detective/directive – manual or automated?

Risks

Internal and external factors that prevent an organization business unit or function from achieving its objectives or strategy.

Data Sources

- External is the kind of data sources that are processed, captured, or acquired from outside the company. This data is not obtained from within the organization.

The drivers of external data sources that need to be considered are economic, social, political, technological, and natural environmental events. Moreover, the sources of this external data are mainly media agency and rating analyst reports, insurance broker assessments, media articles, and much more.

External data sources have four types, which are social media, paid data, open data, and shared data.

- Open information is the kind of data that is freely available for all. There are no restrictions or copyright issues. Anyone can use it or republish it on any platform.
- Paid data is the data that is commercially available. This data needs to be obtained from specialists who have this data. Brokers or marketers can have this data and you can get it by paying some sort of price.
- Shared data is shared between various organizations or companies. This data remains inside the business environment and shared with different entities.
- Social media talks about the data that is shared on social networking websites by its users. Websites like Facebook, LinkedIn, or Twitter can contain this data and it can be used.

- Internal data is acquired and processed from within your firm. The sources of this data are within the company. It can be acquired from different departments, researchers conducted within the company, or documents present in the company. These sources have no connection from the outside world.

The drivers of internal data sources that need to be considered are processes, people, technology, and data. Moreover, the sources of this internal data are generally business budgets and plans, financial litigations, board and annual reports, earlier risk assessments, loss event databases, procedures and policies.

Sales, marketing, finance, as well as human resources are the four major areas of a company that you can use as an internal data source.

- A sales data source is used to determine profit, revenue, and break-even details. Further distribution channels can be analyzed with the help of this data.
- Financial data sources can give you a clear idea of budgeting and expenditure. Cash flow reports can help set budgets and predict future income and expenses.
- Marketing data sources provide insight regarding effective marketing techniques and how well are they being perceived by the target audience. This data can help in the up-gradation of advertising and promotion. Helps the company improve.
- Human resource data sources tell you all about your employees and their issues and disputes. This data can help reduce redundancies and give incentives to improve the output of the process.

Internal Controls

A procedure influenced by an organization's structure, work and authority distribution, employees, and management information system that is aimed at assisting the organization in achieving particular goals or objectives. Risk averted so organization objectives can be achieved. The three main types of internal controls are detective, preventive and corrective.

- Detective Internal Controls

This uncovers an issue or problem in the processes or the operations of the company. This control identifies an undeniable event and analyzes the causes behind it. Join all the pieces of the puzzle to have a complete image.

Examples of detective controls include checking inventory, reviewing reports and documents, and assessing the controls available.

- Preventive Internal Controls

These controls are used to stop an undesirable from occurring. Rather than finding a solution after it has occurred, preventive internal controls prevent a mishap from happening.

Examples of preventive internal controls include keeping check and balance of the applications and machinery, maintaining a correct flow of information, and following all the SOPs.

- Corrective Internal Controls

This is a corrective mechanism. Once the problem is uncovered with the help of detective internal control, corrective internal controls are put in place to make the amends. This is used to fix the problem that has been discovered.

Examples of corrective internal controls include disciplinary action, new policies, filing reports, etc.

Importance of Process Flow

Preparing a process flow for your projects and operations of the company can cut a lot of hassle for you. You have an entire flow available that needs to be followed for all the processes. This saves time and resources too and it can help you concentrate and stay focused. Let's take a deeper look into the importance of process flow.

- Improved quality of your products and services – an imperative – because employees with the best skills set will be assigned a certain task where they can flourish. This gives you enough time to think and choose the perfect strategy and workforce.
- Helps to provide better customer service. Customers are always right, and they are important. With a process flow in front of you, you can easily respond to your customers and maintain your brand image.
- Risk analysis is done effectively, and this can help the company avoid major damages or losses. This helps the management to be prepared from the start and keeps the process smooth and steady.
- A process flow clearly determines unnecessary steps and hindrances that can be avoided in the process. In this way, the entire process can be optimized in a way to improve it.

Review Objectives

- Understand the time, nature, scope, and outcomes of the processes carried out, the evidence gathered, and the conclusions.
- Identify who executed the task and when it was finished.
- Identify who reviewed the work and when they did so.

Examine Objectives to Consider

- Managerial priorities.
- Intents of a commercial and other business nature.
- Changes to the characteristics of processes, goods, and projects.
- The management system needs.
- Contractual and legal obligations to which the organization adheres.
- Whether supplier evaluation is required.
- Expectations and requirements of interested parties, including customers.
- The degree of development of the system.
- What factors might contribute to the enhancement of a management system's effectiveness?
- External demands, such as management system certification.
- Validating compliance with contractual specifications.

- Obtaining and retaining confidence in a supplier's capabilities.
- Assessing the performance of the management system.
- Evaluation of management system objectives' compatibility and alignment with management systems. policy, strategic direction, and corporate objectives as a whole.

End of Module Questions

1. Which of the following is correct about the alignment between risk, objectives, and controls?
   a) There is no need for an alignment.
   b) The alignment depends on your process.
   c) There is only one correct alignment.
   d) None of the above.
2. What are two examples of operational plans?
   a) Corporate and Marketing
   b) Corporate and Contingency
   c) Contingency and Go-to-market
   d) Marketing and Processes
3. What are process owners responsible for?
   a) Developing their process
   b) Improving their process
   c) Outcomes of their process
   d) All of the above
4. What is the correct order of internal reports, from the most general to the most specific?
   a) Routine > Special > Management Level

b) Routine > Management Level > Specific

c) Special > Routine > Management Level

d) Management Level > Special > Routine

5. Is the following statement true or false?
   Internal data sources have no connection whatsoever with the outside of the company.

   a) True

   b) False

6. Which of the following types of internal controls concerns/ concern itself/ themselves with disciplinary actions?

   a) Detective

   b) Preventive

   c) Corrective

   d) Both detective and corrective

7. What is the most important advantage of a structured process flow?

   a) Increased seamlessness of process by removing unnccccssary stcps

   b) Increased time to invest in increasing quality of services

   c) Avoidance of major damages by better risk analysis

   d) Maintenance of brand image by providing better customer service

Module 3: Taking on a New Project

When you've finally begun to build up a client base, and you're regularly taking on new projects, things can get chaotic and quite overwhelming. Making sure that you have a clear and succinct formula for how you plan to go about taking on new clients is absolutely critical toward ensuring success for both your consultancy and your clients.

With that in mind, we're going to use this chapter to outline a few critical strategies that you can use to help ensure a seamless experience when taking on a new project for a client. First, we'll begin with a set of key questions that you'll want to ask your client when taking on a new project. These questions will provide you with critical insight into their thinking process so that you can design the best possible solutions that solve their problems and satisfy their pain points. Let's take a look below.

Learning Outcomes

At the end of this chapter, students are expected to have understood:

- Detailed characteristics of all the pivots of a startup
- Method and importance of developing a strategy
- Procedures of working with startups

Questions You Should Ask Your Client

- In the next one to two years, what do you foresee as the most significant business issues? How can our department's partner accomplish this objective?
- What worked well between our departments in the past should we continue?
- What should we change to be more productive?
- How can we effectively communicate to optimize our collaboration?
- What political concepts should I comprehend as my unit strives to achieve these objectives?
- Who else do you recommend I speak with? Can you link me with them?

Once you're able to generate effective and insightful communications regarding these questions, you can move into the next stage.

So, you've got answers to those key questions, and now it's time to determine just where you come into play as a consultant. Your client has hired you to help them complete a project, accomplish a task, or achieve a goal. With that said, this is your time to show them just what you have to offer.

Take a look below to understand your role in this experience, and to gain some insight into how you'll be evaluated.

How would you like to provide and receive feedback and be updated?

What are your most critical objectives for the year, and how do they align with the strategic goals of the organization?

Describe the two to three most important accomplishments I must attain within a year, and how will I assess them?

What objectives should I set for the next six months?

How can I specifically set you up for success?

One of the ways in which you can better understand your role is to clearly define your consultancy identity. Essentially, you'll want to consider your passions, your skills, your knowledge, and your experience. This will help you develop your core competencies, which you can then use to define your role clearly to potential clients. To establish core competences, a business must take the following steps:

- Isolate its core competencies and develop them into enterprise-wide strengths.
- To guarantee that it is building capabilities that are distinct from those of other organizations, a business must compare itself to those that possess the same competencies.
- Establish an awareness of the features that its clients genuinely value and invest accordingly to build and maintain those capabilities.
- Establish an organizational roadmap with competency development objectives.

- Pursue alliances, acquisitions, and licensing agreements that will enhance the organization's key competencies.
- Encourage organization-wide communication and participation in the development of key capabilities.
- Even when management develops and redefines the business, it is imperative to maintain the company's fundamental competencies.
- Outsource or liquidate non-core assets to free up resources for expanding key competencies.

Learn About Startups

A growing and expanding medium of exchange in the online world. The largest online shoe store in the world has annual sales of $1 billion. Startups are businesses that are in the first stage of their operations. At this point, a startup is being funded by the entrepreneurial founders of the company. These are young companies that come up with an idea of a unique and new product or service to cater to the news of the market.

Startups are high-risk businesses because of their newness in the industry. There are no specific types of companies that fall into the category of startups. Any company with these features can be a startup. Startups turn into proper companies and businesses when they achieve a certain size, receive a high level of revenue, attract enough investments or become a public company.

- Cohort Analysis

This is a behavior analysis in which users with similar characteristics are grouped to understand their actions and behavior towards your products and services. Customer behavior sequences known as flows are crucial to this process. They control how buyers engage with a business's goods.

- Lean Manufacturing Principle of Kanban

This is workflow management that defines, manages, and improves the entire manufacturing process. This principle aims to visualize the entire workflow and then maximize the productivity and efficiency of the company. This principle provides structure and stability to your workflow. The lean principle decreases waste activities without negatively impacting the production levels.

The goal of this method is to increase the value of customers without increasing the cost. A professional Kanban board is made to track the processes and operations of the business, maximize efficiency, and manage the entire project. The features of a Kanban board are:

- Backlog

These are the things mentioned in the first column which your project manager may or may not deliver. This is a list of ideas which you should work on to make them happen.

- In Progress

As the word suggests, these are the projects that were selected by your project manager and the work has been started on these. These projects are in progress.

- Built

This is the column where the projects or tasks that are completed are listed down. All the projects that are completed and no further work is needed to be done are mentioned in this column of the Kanban board.

- Validated

Validated is the last column and in this column, a validation analysis is done in which the project manager analyzes whether it was wise to undertake the project at all.

The number of potential pivots made is known as the startup runway (i.e., how long a startup has before it runs out of moncy, calculated by dividing its current cash on hand by its monthly operating expenses).

Some pivots are listed below.

- Concentrate-pivot

The entirety of a product is reduced to a single feature. Everything else in the product is not included and cut away. Moreover, this is the driving force in retaining the focus of the organization in delivering the product with minimum but enough features to the market.

- Dissipate-pivot

The entirety of a product is affected by a single feature. This pivot is the complete opposite of zoom-in-pivot. This pivot is used by the companies when the data shows that the features of the product are not enough for it to be launched in the market.

- Customer-segment-pivot

This pivot is used to reposition the product when the product attracts real customers but is not in accordance with its actual vision. This pivot helps optimize the product and make it more appreciative in the market segment.

- Customers-need-pivot

Customers might have many problems with the product but that doesn't mean all the problems are valid and worth paying for. This pivot helps the product team to identify an actual problem that is worth solving and paying for.

- Platform

Changing from a platform to an application or vice versa. As the word literally suggests, many managers believe that the product they are providing can be a platform for potential future products.

- Business-architecture-pivot

The two major business architectures are the complicated model of the system (low volume, high margin) and the model of volume operations (high volume, low margin). The pivot identified that no business could do both models at the same time.

- Value-capture-pivot

This pivot focuses on monetization and the revenue generation model. This talks about capturing value through the product. Not only capture but also increase the overall revenue.

- The engine-of-growth pivots

There are three engines of growth pivots that are discussed in detail later in the module. Viral, sticky, and paid growth models. These models help the company increase sales and profitability.

- Channel-pivot

This pivot refers to the delivery system or the channel of delivering the product. The pivot identifies a more effective and efficient way of delivering the product to the target audience. This pivot impacts the pricing and advertising of the product.

- Technology-pivot

When companies find a better and different technology to provide the same solution, they make this pivot. This provides better price or performance which in return improves the competitive position of the company.

The Wisdom of the Five Whys

Describe your business in five ways. This is considered a brainstorming technique in which you continuously ask the question 'why.' The number five has no significant importance as you can find the answer less than five times. This is a way to find the root cause of the problem or the issue at hand. Once the problem and the root cause are clear to the team, everyone can give input to find a suitable solution.

The Key to Working with Startups

Were you recently contacted by a startup? Well, that's a good thing. They likely recognize your skills and expertise, and they believe that your services would be an asset to their growth and development. Working with a startup isn't exactly an easy task. In reality, it can be quite challenging, but with the right strategy, you can ensure a successful experience.

Startups require an effective strategy for a fine plan and rigorous market research. You should work with your client to help them identify the right target audience for their products, services, or solutions. Additionally, vision/concept, product development, marketing/sales, scaling up, partnerships/distribution, and structure/organizational design are all areas that should be tackled early on.

In the face of such daunting uncertainty, your plan must include a means of tracking your advancement. When to get it done; when to collaborate; when to engage with feedback;

when to remain with the goal; and how and when to invest in expanding the business are just some of the numerous trade-off decisions that can be clarified by this framework for entrepreneurs.

In the early days, our main concerns deal with:

- For whom and what should we construct this?
- We need to know what market we can enter and eventually conquer.
- How can we create long-lasting value that is immune to market forces?

One idea would be to launch a poor first product, day-one pricing, and revenue goals based on tiny amounts of money brought in as a strategy to force accountability are all examples of this.

Testing the Product/Service

The value-hypothesis and the growth-hypothesis, as I've coined them, are the two most crucial assumptions we business owners make. The value-hypothesis examines whether or not a service or good actually benefits its users. What factors suggest staff members value volunteer work? A comparable analysis can be used to assess the growth-hypothesis, which hypothesizes how new customers would learn about a product or service. How will the software expand from its early adopters to the rest of the staff once it's up and running?

1. Have you established that the general public understands they have the issue your product intends to address?
2. Would they pay for a solution if it existed?
3. If we offered it, would they buy it?
4. Is there anything we can do to fix it?

We shouldn't assume acceptance and usage of it.

Innovation Accounting

Start by creating a minimum viable product (MVP) to gather accurate information about the current state of the business. You can't start keeping tabs on your progress toward a goal if you don't have a clear image of where you stand right now, no matter how far away you may be.

Second, new businesses need to work on fine-tuning their engines so that they perform as well as possible. The tipping point for a startup comes when it has completed all the little adjustments and product optimizations necessary to shift its baseline closer to the ideal.

Third, axis or perseverance.

Three Growth Factors

Sticky Growth Factor

By keeping an eye on the churn rate, which is the percentage of consumers who stop using the service or product over a given time frame, the product will expand if the rate of gaining new customers is higher than the rate of losing existing ones. Sticky engine can be taken at face value because it makes it difficult for customers to abandon a product and attracts a small number of new ones.

Viral Growth Factor

Utilizing your current clientele to raise awareness of your product or service is essential for expansion. The viral engine retains existing consumers and increases engagement, resulting in an increase in recommendations. Referrals assist the company to promote its goods to the current customer's friends and coworkers.

Paid Growth Factor

What is the cost of obtaining a new consumer, and how much revenue will that customer bring? This is a way to increase your customer base by paying to market your products. In this method, companies use paid ads on websites and social networking sites to target more customers. The cost increases as the target market gets more segmented.

Developing a Strategy

1. Where are we? Discuss where we are in the partnership. Examine how you got there. What has gone well and what hasn't?
2. Where do we wish to go? What would generate the most profit if all obstacles were removed? What is realistic and what is aspiration? Prioritize and come back.

3. What modifications must be made? Contrast the existing state with the desired condition. What's limiting you? What do you need to stop or start doing? What would it take to get the results we want?

4. How must these modifications be made? It won't be quick. There are actions we can perform that will yield quick benefits, but we will need to convince others to follow the approach. How will we get their support intellectually and emotionally?

5. How do you measure progress? Don't get too hung up on measurement. Demonstrate progress that brings the plans to life.

Furthermore, developing a strategy can still be a little tricky and to make it a little less complicated what you need to do is measure the business case against something comparable. After this, you need to identify mistakes, problems, and risks. This is a very important stage because such issues can sabotage your strategy easily. After you have identified them, you need to find solutions. You need to propose smart solutions that are doable and protect the company.

The last thing that you need to do is to educate yourself more about everything. Having awareness regarding the ins and outs of a startup and how the company works is very important. This helps you have a better knowledge of the market and process all the operations smoothly.

Importance of Developing a Strategy

It is hard for all businesses to get it right at the start and especially for start-ups. Every organization has its weaknesses which can be hard to overcome but a perfect strategy can help you overcome all these issues. Let's talk about the importance of developing a strategy.

- The strategy works as a guide for the management. It highlights how the business is performing internally and how competitive it is with its rivals. It gives an idea about the internal and external performance of the company.
- The strategy also gives a clearer view and a vision for the business to follow. When a strategy is developed the goals become achievable and smart. It becomes a sense of direction for all the people in the company.
- The strategy works best to predict and identify patterns and trends in the future. Strategies can examine changes in the market and give a clearer view of future opportunities. Future market predictions can help you strategize accordingly.
- Lastly, developing a strategy provides a competitive advantage over competitors of the company. The company outperforms its competitors and has a better understanding of themselves and where they are going in the future.

Now that you've got a wealth of information related to working with a new client, taking on a new project, and developing a strategy for a startup, it's time to move into another new chapter.

Every consultant can benefit from working within a team setting. From time to time, you may take on a new client that has asked more of you than any client has previously – this is a good thing.

In these cases, it allows you to serve as a liaison between other consultants just like you, who maintain their vast expertise in their fields and specializations.

When you're able to effectively build a team, bring them all together, and bring forth a comprehensive and holistic solution for your client, you present yourself as a one-stop-shop, and that's all that any client could ever ask for.

In the next chapter, let's talk more about team building and how it relates to your process as a consultant.

End of Module Questions

Module 4: Meeting with Your Team

When it comes time to expand your consultancy and bring in a team of professionals to help ensure that you have the right level of knowledge, skill, and expertise to meet the demands of your clients, you need to know how to manage that relationship. In this short chapter, we're going to talk about a few best practices to help you build a well-functioning team that has the necessary level of expertise to provide added value for your clients.

We're going to begin with some basic team-building tips and strategies that you can use to foster the right company culture within your consultancy. Let's begin with team meetings. First off, how often should you have them? How long should they be? How many people should they include? And of course, what should you talk about during these meetings? Let's take a look down below.

Learning Outcomes

At the end of this chapter, students are expected to have understood:

- Types of meetings in an organization
- Importance of team meetings
- Tips for conducting effective team meetings
- Characteristics of one-page briefs

Whole Team Meetings

One of the best ways to connect with your team is to hold an 'all-staff' meeting in which all of your team members gather together once a week to discuss your trajectory.

In these meetings, you can talk about business in general, or you can follow up and plan out specific projects in which your entire team is involved. However, it is always recommended to keep these meetings to just once a week. Allow your teams to report back with meaningful information and impactful results. Meetings can be conducted in many ways. You can keep team meetings or one-to-one individual meetings. All this depends on the purpose of the meeting and the people involved in that.

The duration of the meetings also depends on you, moreover, it's up to you to hold these meetings daily, weekly, fortnightly, or monthly. Before making all these decisions, you need to look at all the aspects beforehand and then finalize a verdict.

Individuals

On an individual basis, it's a good idea to meet with your staff separately about two or three times a week. With frequent meetings, you can keep things short and simple, but just long enough to gain a glimpse of what people are working on. From there, you can provide feedback and next steps, so that you can ensure a successful outcome on whatever project(s) they've signed.

Cadence Meeting

Cadence meetings are regular meetings with the team. These meetings are short and frequent, and they are held to motivate the employees. Moreover, these meetings also increase the momentum and efficiency of the employees. The longer meetings are less frequent, and they are between the board members in which different ideas and insights are pitched in.

This is a platform given to the employees to share their views, ideas, and information with the team leader and other senior members of the company.

    o   Weekly Team

Your weekly team cadence meeting is similar to your weekly all-staff meeting. In the cadence meeting, you'll want to discuss current projects and project trajectories. Take a look down below for some tips.

- Report global updates and status of the entire project status.
- Set weekly goals and follow up on task assignments.

Raise any concerns with hitting deadlines.

    o   Individual Daily

Along with individual meetings, you can hold individual daily cadence meetings. These should be kept very short and last no longer than ten minutes, maximum. Take a look down below to learn about what these meetings should consist of:

- Checking in with the progress of tasks
- Creative lead: giving feedback
- Flagging any issues that might make you miss a deadline
- Having them post dailies for creative review

Importance of Team Meetings

Team meetings are very important on a regular basis and if done effectively these can hold great importance. Some of the reasons why team meetings hold such great importance are listed below.

- Employee Engagement

Employees have a platform to engage with all the members of the company and they feel that their opinion is considered and valuable. These meetings motivate employees and help them value their job. As employee engagement increases, the overall productivity of the company increases and benefits the business.

- A Platform for Innovation and Creative Thinking

These meetings are a platform for the members of the business to critically think and come up with innovative ideas.

The feeling that they are being heard motivates them to showcase their creative side. Teamwork and meetings can turn a good idea into a master plan.

- Improved Decision-making Process

When there are more people brainstorming solutions for any issue, it is easier to come up with a quick solution. More team members mean ample information to solve a problem that the company is facing. Team members can have better insight into the issue and can provide more visibility to the managers. The entire decision-making process is made quick and effective through these meetings.

- Stronger Relationships

Personal interaction builds up stronger relationships. A good team has strong communication between them and these meetings promote good communication. These meetings strengthen bonds between the employees which further increases productivity and efficiency.

- Promotes Inclusion

When these meetings become routine, the culture of these meetings becomes encouraging and inclusive. Employees feel that they are being heard for their ideas and their insight is important. No one is judged or treated differently because of any reason. It is important to create an encouraging environment for everyone to share their ideas and thoughts in these meetings.

- Channel for Continuous Feedback

Meetings are an immediate way of feedback because they are face-to-face. This sort of open communication allows the employees of the company to grow professionally. These meetings make the employees learn how to improve themselves professionally. They can together analyze the ongoing situation and work on the future of the company and its employees.

Tips for Conducting Effective Team Meetings

Any business owner or manager can conduct team meetings in their company but not all of those can be effective. Team meetings need to be effective to gain maximum out of them and further increase the business's productivity. Here are some tips that can help you make your team meetings effective and productive.

- Determine Meeting Attendees

The attendees of the meeting should be decided according to the purpose of the meeting. The employees who are not related to the operations department should not be invited to an operations department meeting. Before deciding the attendees, ask yourself who will provide better insight on a certain issue and who can benefit from this meeting.

- Have a Clear Agenda

Before deciding anything, you need to set the purpose and the agenda of the meeting straight. List down the things you want to talk about and the issues you want to resolve in the meeting. Also, note down the predicted outcomes of the meeting which can help you move the meeting in the right direction.

- Stick to the Agenda

When you are surrounded by a team of professionals, it's very hard to not stay on one topic. With so many ideas you can easily go off-track. As a manager or business owner, it's your job to stick to the agenda and purpose of the business. Keep the members engaged on the agenda and find answers to the questions being asked in the agenda.

- Prepare a Schedule

Set meetings beforehand and give the attendees of the meeting enough time to prepare and schedule other matters of the business accordingly. Schedule your meeting in a way that everything on the agenda is discussed and given its fair share of time. Make sure nothing is missed and wrap your meetings up in the given time. If the meeting is over before time, then don't drag it and end it.

- Endorse Feedback

As a team manager, it's your core responsibility to give fair and equal chances to everyone to speak and give their insights in the meeting. Your team members' input can give more ideas and options to ponder upon. There is no harm in getting ample ideas so let them use this platform and make these meetings effective.

- Note Action Items

Last but not the least, note down all the important things discussed in the meeting. These action items should be documented by someone and then implemented and acted upon. These are important as these are the inputs of the members, and you need to follow up on these. They can be forgotten or misplaced if not documented properly.

One-Page Creative Brief

A creative brief is a clear document that is aligned with the objectives of the projects and the goals that the company aims to achieve. This document outlines the strategy that the company needs to follow to get the project done. This brief gives a complete vision of the brand or the project the company is working on. This brief includes goals, purpose, target audience, tasks, and other key information.

Goal

What is the goal and context of the project? Keep the goal short and clear – one line. For example, "Create a Real Estate brochure that will help real-estate brokers communicate to potential clients." A goal is an objective that you want to achieve. You need to mention a goal in your creative brief so that you can have a clear idea of what you will be working on.

Target Audience

Who is going to see this (demographic)? What are their challenges? Why do they care? "Real estate broker who is having a hard time telling a story of a new development." The people who will be using your product or service. The target audience is your consumer base or market for whom this product will be launched. The product or service will cater to the needs of the target audience.

Creative Parameters and Considerations

This is a creative sandbox for your team to play in. Room for interpretation; any solution is valid within these bounds. Be careful of vague words; make sure it's clear but not too boxed in. These are the boundaries within which you can play around. There's no one solution for a problem but the right solution is always one. So, all the solutions and ideas that are given to achieve a goal should be bound by some parameters and considerations.

Checklists

Binary dos and don'ts. This is like a to-do list that helps a business keep a record of all the things that need to be done along with a deadline to get those things done. A checklist helps you stay on the timeline and achieve consistency. Mandates for the project.

References

Supporting information or reference is always a good option because it can help others understand the concept in a better way. Types of references used in a creative brief are:

- Documents
- Links
- Video
- Articles
- Websites

Milestones

Keeping track of all your important and due dates is essential. You need to track your projects and the stages they are on according to the timeline that is set. For this purpose, milestones are set to check how the project is going on. All important dates to hit on the project, project deliveries, client postings, project phases/rounds.

Delivery Specs

- Video (60sec.mov file, ProRes Codec, 1920x1080 resolution, at 24fps, in SRGB color)
- Brochure (8 pages, PDF, 8.5x11", with 0.125" bleed in CMYK color).

Tailor the creative brief for each team member, define their roles and expectations – your expectation of what, by when.

In the next chapter, we're going to talk a bit more about what you can do to use what you've built so far to properly engage with clients before, during, and after you begin working with them. As a consultant, your role will change and fluctuate throughout the lifespan of a project – from advising to innovating, to designing, and to problem-solving, you'll do it all.

Knowing how to navigate these changes and fluctuations will be the difference-maker when it comes to a satisfied client and an unsatisfied client. Let's move into the next chapter and shed some light on just what your client engagements should look like, feel like, and end like.

End of Module Questions

Module 5: Engaging with Client

When engaging with your clients, you'll need to be able to put together a range of services, solutions, and support systems to ensure that you're targeting and satisfying their every need. With that in mind, the nature of consulting revolves around a spinning, changing, and ever-evolving set of requirements that you'll likely need to embrace throughout the lifespan of a project.

While you might clearly define your role when you first begin working with a client, that role will likely change and fluctuate over time. This is by design – you want to be responsive to your client's needs during the development of a project, and you certainly don't want to come across as too rigid. When your client asks for something, they'll be counting on you to deliver.

In this chapter, we're going to take a deep dive into just how you can go about engaging with your clients. Let's start with some prerequisites.

Learning Outcomes

At the end of this chapter, students are expected to have understood:

- Steps of client engagement
- Strategies of client engagement
- How to present your work to the clients?

Pre-requisites

Prerequisites are essentially the must-haves that you need to bring to the table when engaging with your clients. They will often revolve around simply getting to know what your client has in mind first. Listen to their words, hear their ideas, and try to organize and streamline this information for them in a way that is digestible, clearly articulated, and actionable. In other words, you need insights that you can act upon to bring about the right solution – so, start the project by ensuring that you and your client are on the very same page.

The discovery process is a fun one because it involves a lot of client interaction. Here, you'll have the opportunity to brainstorm with your clients, bounce ideas off of one another, and share prior projects that worked for previous clients.

We always recommend that you set the collaborative process in the right direction from the outside in. Transfer ideas to design, moving along a set of sequential steps. Use style-scapes to agree on design directions, and keep the client apprised of where you're headed.

The design stage really takes flight once you hand over your first draft or first iteration of a potential solution. Here, your client gets to gain a deeper understanding of what you're actually bringing to the table. And in the same breath, you get the chance to really focus on what your client is ultimately looking for.

No project is successful after just one try – so don't try to be perfect. Instead, focus on the task, and simply try to land on a good starting point that you can build off of.

Presenting the Work

So, once you've got something to show your client, where do you begin? How do you get started? How do you show it to them? Well, there are a variety of ways in which you can present the work.

For instance, you can do it in person. You can schedule a teleconference if the client isn't local or you can simply mail them a finished product or prototype and communicate remotely. But no matter what, always remember that presenting the work is better than submitting the final copy unannounced.

Identify design jobs (selling the client on a single concept) are best presented in person. Make sure all decision-makers are in the room before you present; record it. Clients shouldn't see anything until you formally make your presentation. Don't give clients something that is not complete, or you don't have complete knowledge of. This can have a very negative impression on your clients. So much so that you can even lose a client because of inadequate information or less effort.

Show Incredible Work

Start at the Beginning – recap the reason for the new identity. Example, "Our goal is to build a new visual identity" that (Objective/Point -> for approvals -> context -> client ideas and point).

Recap the steps you have taken together. Remind them of the place they were in when they were giving you this inspiration. It's difficult for people to disagree with other people and even more difficult to disagree with themselves.

"Power Cleaner – Build on the steps you have already taken, so everybody's on the same page."

Avoid remarks like, "What do you think?"

"How did we do?"

Go for – "Did we take a step in the right direction?"

"Are we completely off the mark?"

"What would others think?"

Display your work by explaining your thoughts behind each version. Have a story. Is this story better told visually? Look to show the relationship between each piece designed and the element of inspiration. Manage and control revisions. Set deadlines and meet expectations.

Steps towards Client Engagement

As mentioned above, engaging the client is essential and there are some prerequisites for client engagement. This not only helps you to understand the project, but the client is also satisfied. The client is well-aware of the working practices of your company and devises a plan that suits both parties. Let's look at all the steps that you should be aware of, and you should follow these when engaging with a client.

- Be a Good Listener

If you are a business owner or manager, that doesn't mean that you should be the one talking. It is very important for the client to feel heard. Moreover, you don't want to make mistakes in between the projects so it's better to listen to the instructions attentively. There are few things that you need to keep in mind when engaging with a client.

- Concentrate – make efforts to focus on what the speaker is saying.
- Acknowledge – show your presence by nodding or verbally showing.
- Respond – ask questions during the process to clear out any ambiguities.
- Empathize – understand the point of view and feelings of the client.

These characteristics make you a better listener and that positively impacts the client, you, and your business.

- Ask Questions

There is no harm in asking questions because questions are for the better understanding of both you and the client. Asking personal questions might be a better idea here rather than asking sales-related questions. The questions can't be too personal but something that the client can talk about without any hesitance.

- Keep Conversing

As mentioned in previous points, listening and speaking are very important. So, have a conversation with your client rather than having a formal meeting with your client. Make the conversation friendly so that it becomes more effective. Have casual conversations and make the engagement better.

- Suitable Content

The content of this informal meeting is vital. You need to see if the content being used in the meeting is fulfilling your motives for this conversation. Set the goals of this conversation before it starts and align your content with your objectives.

- Body Language

Body language plays a huge role in determining the flow and outcome of the conversation. Make sure that your body language lines up with what you say. Eye contact or hand gestures put weight in what you say and show that you have an interest in having this conversation.

- Adjust Your Style

The style of the client is something you need to be aware of or you need to figure out at the start of these conversations. Adjusting to their style gives you an edge because clients like it when they are treated the way they want to be. If your client requires extra details, then adjust to this and give more detail.

- Simplicity

It's better to make your client understand your point rather than showing off your fancy vocabulary. If you are using words that are not commonly used just to impress your client and they don't get it, then they might be reluctant in having any further conversation with you. So, keep your conversations simple and understandable. You need to bond with the client, not show off.

- Integrity

Don't say things to butter your client. Say the things that you mean and stick to the things that you tell your client. Clients can easily sense insecurity and lack of credibility, so it's your duty to maintain the trust and faith of the client. Show them that you and your company are credible and the best for their job.

- Be Prepared

You have to be prepared to answer the questions being asked by the client and provide what they need on the spot. The client might not have a lot of time so try to summarize your points quickly and present them to the client for a final and clear understanding. Clients can throw any sort of query or question so keep all the information with you and be prepared.

- Review Your Writing

Any sort of document being shared with the client or even an exchange of email can go wrong if you don't thoroughly review your writings. Check all your work and send it after proofreading and reviewing. Make sure you are clear, your tone is suitable, and the client will be able to understand the text without you explaining it to them. There is no room for misunderstanding or error.

- Not Only About Selling

Don't jump in to sell your product or service only. Start the conversation to get to know the client and have a conversation to build a relationship. Once you believe that enough has been shared, that is when you should introduce your product or service and then move to the selling part.

All these steps are applicable in any situation, whether you are in a conference room with a sales situation, a lunch meeting, or a virtual call. You need to know how to engage with your client and have effective communication. Engaging is all about building a relationship with your client and converting it into sales later on.

Client Engagement Strategies for Your Business

A client engagement strategy is a way or a plan to increase the satisfaction of the client by communicating with them. This involves building a relationship with the client to understand them in a better way and convey your message in an even better way. These strategies can be implemented online, in-person, over a phone call, or via virtual video calls. These strategies help us make our client engagement proactive from reactive. Some of the strategies are listed below.

- Engage Through Diverse Channels

Engaging with your clients through various channels can help you build a reputation that you are responsive. It can be time-consuming, but clients will be happy getting information when they need it and from wherever they need it. Use all your platforms and be responsive and ready to assist your valuable clients. This increases client engagement.

- Share Your Reviews

Thanking your clients publicly can boost your reputation and image of your company. If you get a review on Google or Yelp, just share it on your online platforms and thank your clients. This will increase client engagement and motivate other clients to give reviews and connect with you.

- Check Your Silent Clients

Not everyone is vocal about their experiences but that doesn't mean that they shouldn't be noticed. Keep a check on your shy folks and give them acknowledgements because this would mean a lot to them, and they would feel special. This will also be an opportunity to increase engagement with them and give them some room to talk to them further.

- Reward Engagement

Giveaways and gift packages can be sent to your clients to appreciate their active engagement. This is a great gesture as they will be flattered to receive these goodies and probably announce them on their social media. This is how you can keep your clients happy and boost further engagement with clients.

- Use the Feedback

Listening is vital in a business and giving proper attention to the feedback of your clients can help your business. Every client has their own perspective and feedback and as a business owner, it's your job to take this under consideration. Working and implementing feedback can make the clients believe in you and your principles. Because of quick responses, they will engage more since they feel important.

- Stick to Your Word

Keeping promises in your business is the principle that you can't say no to. Stories of great customer service are made from sticking to your word and delivering what you have promised. Make sure that the promise in your promotional campaign lines up with your final product. Sticking to your word gives a boost to positive engagement.

- Involve Customers in Social Cause

Social cause is always the right way to attract legitimate customers and make the entire image of your company better. Clients want to feel good about their money and if there is a social aspect to your product, then they are eager to spend money. You can provide volunteer opportunities to your clients so that they can work with your employees on social projects. This increases the overall engagement of your client with the entire company.

- Use the Data

As a business, you might be collecting data in the form of surveys and questionnaires. This data can play a major role if this is used for the right reasons. You can also get data from the consumer pattern and understand the pattern behind the kinds of products your clients use. This can improve the customer experience and overall client engagement.

End of Module Questions

Module 6: Updates Are Critical

Don't forget, when you're working for a client, it's best that you keep them updated on your progress because they went out of their way to hire you. They're still likely interested in having at least somewhat of a say in the progression of the project.

Always be sure that you're keeping them up-to-date on your progress. They may want to change things along the way, and they may even have a new idea that they'd like you to build off of. With that said, here are a few tips to remember.

Learning Outcomes

At the end of this chapter, students are expected to have understood:

- Advantages of updating your clients
- Why are client updates important for a business?
- How to update your clients through reports?

Benefits of Client Updates

1. Makes your clients feel at ease. This gives them the satisfaction that they are being a part of the entire project. When they are constantly being told about their progress, they don't doubt your capabilities. They have faith in your company and this belief helps your company to grow. A good word or recommendation is given by these clients to more people who are looking for similar services. This increases your client base.

2. Puts you on top of things always. You can easily communicate with them and get their insights so if anything is not going according to the plan, the client can tell you. This helps you a lot. When the communication is so frequent then there are fewer chances of error and repetitive issues. You can understand the needs of clients in a better way.

3. Build trust in your team due to transparency. Everyone is aware of the operations happening in the project. Nothing is hidden from any party which makes it better for trust and confidence. Trust and confidence are the keys to success and a team needs to have these. This helps everyone to work efficiently and perform for the same cause. A team like this goes a long way and thrives for success.

4. Let them know that things are still moving. They know the situation of the project and the stages it is on. Keep them in the loop. Keeping your clients in the loop is what you want. You want them to have an idea

of the entire process that nothing catches them with surprise. Surprise elements can turn into bad shocks in no time. Keeping them in the loop gives you the ease and satisfaction that they know how the project is going.

Why Updating Your Clients Is Important

Maintaining regular communication with your clients is important to build the trust of clients that their work is your top priority. Apart from building trust, communicating with the client allows you to avoid minor issues and reservations of clients in any step of the project. This will lead to clear misunderstandings and prevent simple issues into big troubles.

To Ensure the Transparency

Updating the status of all steps of the project you are handling ensures transparency. With regular updating, you can make sure that you are completing each task without skipping important things.

To Schedule WIP postings

The WIP tool is usually used in the construction industry which gives an update about the progress of contracts on to assigned time. WIP refers to the Work in Process to give an assessment of the progress of projects to your clients. Through WIP reporting you can provide the schedule of work you had made for completed projects and the schedule of running projects. Usually, the WIP schedule contains the following columns:

- Total cost to complete the projects
- Calculation of gross profit
- Billings till now
- Price of contract
- Costs incurred to date

The WIP postings enable clients to oversee how their company is handling the work. The WIP postings allow you to monitor the total cost, profits, and other cost adjustments when needed.

To Educate Your Clients

Some clients may not be well aware of the latest trends, tools, operations, and actual reasons behind the successful completion of projects. It's your duty to educate your clients about your key strategies of good performance, trends in the industry.

For example, you can talk about the market focus, trends in digital integration of businesses, and current talents in the market. This will make it easy for you to justify the reason if you have done changes in projects.

To Demonstrate Your Success

To build the trust of clients on your team it's important that your clients must realize you are accomplishing tasks successfully. If your clients will not realize that you are achieving success, then it's quite possible that your efforts will be taken for granted or not even noticed. So, update your clients about significant results.

If the client has asked to change specific things or highlighted problem areas after successfully resolving highlighted issues, update the clients to let them know how effectively you have resolved errors.

To Hold Your Clients Accountable

Sometimes problems may happen if you are not provided with the priorities of clients properly and clients may not take action on providing things you need on behalf of the client. If you are getting in touch with clients regularly you can easily address these issues.

Clients will realize where the actual problem occurred. Keeping clients accountable will let you resolve misunderstandings that may be based on changing goals. Sometimes clients may have reservations about your performance.

Updating clients with key performance indicators and detailed metrics hold them accountable when you relate your results with the information provided by your clients.

Updating Clients by Giving Reports

Updating clients by giving reports refers to reporting about the overview of the project, i.e., how you are handling their projects, and how much work is done so far. Making changes in a project after completion according to a review of the client is time-consuming and a bad impression of project handling as well. You have to stay updated regarding the priorities of clients, this will lead to fewer errors and editing on the work that you have done. So, to avoid this tedious situation it's important to give updates about every step of the project you are working on.

Updating clients in the form of a formal report is the best strategy to maintain professional practices and to build the confidence of the client in you. Your reports must be comprehensible, well written so that clients will easily understand what you want to deliver.

Essentials of Client Reports

As a consulting business strategist, you must know the important sections that you should include while giving updates to your clients. You must include the following sections in the client report.

Monthly Summary

Updating your client by monthly summary refers to reporting your client about accomplished work and the ongoing status of the project. You can communicate about your achievements and the pace of ongoing work. This will give confidence to the client about your recent performance and productivity level as well.

A monthly summary must be compiled on the listing of major activities and how much you have worked on them, and what are your goals for the upcoming month. It ensures the client that your company has set challenging goals to complete the tasks effectively.

To ensure that your monthly summary has played an important role in communicating with your client, you have to follow some basic guidelines. Write a title and label focusing on the type of report, date of report, the time covered by the report, and name of the department or team who are working on it.

Giving the project management and progress report in a monthly summary is the best opportunity to budget changing requests and other things you need from a client.

Dashboards

Giving updates to your client in the form of a dashboard means giving an analytical report through compiling data, in graphical form. Updates by dashboards usually focus on performance metrics, the status of work, and the prediction of how much work your team will complete.

When all metrics are monitored, the client will know what kind of goals the company will achieve and how it will affect the projects in the short or long term. Dashboards make it easy for your clients to understand the information without reading and analyzing any lengthy written piece.

Research Reports

Research reports mean updating your clients about the hypothesis, summary of findings, methodology, and conclusion of the study to receive positive results. The client may be impressed by your research and will act on it. This is the best way to demonstrate the value of your services for the business of the client.

Industry Report and Forecast

Updating your clients about the relevant industry can give them in-depth knowledge about the latest trends in the market, the size of the market, forecasts, and competitors in the market. This will help your clients in making strategic decisions.

How to Prepare Reports to Update the Clients

To update your clients about work progress and other necessary factors which are important to address, you must know how to prepare a formal report. You have to prepare reports according to the preferences of every client. These are some of the important factors while preparing a report.

Creating a Questionnaire

Creating a questionnaire in a report will sort out the exact goals of your client, and how much your client is satisfied with your work so far. Create a questionnaire focusing on finding how your clients are experiencing your services, and whether your clients are happy with any new service you are offering.

Apart from your performance, and efforts also ask about the pricing of your services. Here are the key questions you should ask from your client:

- What can my team do to serve you better?
- To what extent are you satisfied with our services?
- What is the major advantage you gained from our services?
- What are your basic challenges to achieve growth this year?

Indicate Measure of Performance by KPIs and Metrics

Prepare an analytical presentation of your performance indicating how your team is achieving the goals. Your KPIs (Key Performance Indicators) should include:

Quality: You should focus on how well the project is executed. How your efforts improved the standard of the project?

Timeliness: Mention the deadline given by the client and how much you have worked on a specific project to meet the deadlines. Define your targets to ensure your completion of tasks on time.

Budget: Mention the calculation of expenses and the total amount you need to complete the project.

Effectiveness: Focus on how you are doing efforts to increase productivity and how you are utilizing money and time for successful results.

Metrics are vital aspects to update clients. Design metrics intending to express and measure the status of work. Metrics should monitor your performances, effectiveness of strategies.

In the final chapter, we're going to provide you with some clear-cut consulting strategies to ensure that you have everything you need to hit the ground running once you're ready to begin taking on new clients.

End of Module Question

Module 7: Consulting Strategies

Any effective consultant has several critical strategies up his or her sleeve that they can use when working with clients. Often, these strategies revolve around critical management and business metrics that help to provide your clients with critical insight into performance, cause, and effect, and so much more.

In this chapter, we'll show you a variety of tools and strategies that you can use to demonstrate your expertise and to test the validity and efficacy of your solutions.

Learning Outcomes

At the end of this chapter, students are expected to have understood:

- Importance of scorecard
- Features and benefits of benchmarking
- Process of rethinking and changing strategies

Root-Cause Analysis

Throughout the week, everyone on the team should log any problems encountered. At the end of the week, the biggest most recurring problem will be discussed. This is a process through which the root causes of a problem are identified. If the problem is repeated, then the pattern is identified, and all the trigger points are sorted out. After the analysis, appropriate solutions are given out to curb that issue.

Just analyzing the issue doesn't solve the problem, finding out a viable solution is as important as the analysis.

Observations

1. Confine yourself to a narrow sphere of observation, so similar opportunities present themselves.
2. Those similar opportunities enable you to see the patterns.
3. Observations emerge as you notice the patterns, articulate the insight, and apply the findings in your speaking, writing, and advising.

There is no intelligence without pattern matching; there is no pattern matching without similar circumstances; and there are no identical circumstances without a strict positioning. This will form the basis of everything you do.

Think independently in order to be more intelligent than others.

1. Develop an information advantage:

a) Develop meaningful interactions with individuals who have achieved the same objectives as you.

b) Gain knowledge from various disciplines and apply the knowledge to your own.

c) Construct a laboratory, not a study.

2. Invest also in what will not change instead of what will change. Bottom line is that you have to dig in and become the greatest in one prominent business by constantly investing in it throughout time, as opposed to leaping from one trend to the next and starting all over again.

3. Use storytelling to make the vision more compelling.

   a) Retreat

       Pick a notepad and select a place devoid of daily disturbances in which you may write. Meditate and write whatever you have been feeling or the ideas that keep coming to your mind. Make a story out of it and pen it all down in a comfortable environment.

   b) Visualize

       Imagine your desired life in five years. Have this image in your head of where you want to be in the next five years or what goals you have to achieve in this timespan. Having a clear image can help you a lot in living this dream.

   c) Ask

       You need to ask yourself questions to achieve these objectives and to make your dream come true. These questions help you make your goals specific, measurable, achievable, realistic, and team bound.

- What is your premium revenue?
- How many individuals comprise your team?
- How would your employees characterize your organization's culture to a family member?
- What are the media saying about your company? Be as particular as possible. What would your local newspaper report about your business? What would your preferred publication say?
- What do you appreciate most about your company's vision, and where is it headed?
- How would a client characterize their interaction with your company? What would they tell their closest companion?
- Which achievements are you most pleased with? What achievement is your population most proud of?
- What is it that you accomplish better than anyone else on earth?
- Define your office atmosphere in detail.
- Specify your area of expertise. Who are your clients, and what do they think?
- What sort of message do you try to give through your promotions and techniques? How does your target audience perceive that brand message?

Fair Scorecard

The fair scorecard is a system for monitoring key areas of a company's strategy and supporting organizational change or improvement. It examines parameters beyond normal financial measurements to assist businesses in focusing on their long-term strategic objectives and spotting potential problems before they surface in the financial statements.

The scorecard is an exhaustive list of quantifiable goals that may be measured throughout time. Common features include:

- Revenue
- Customer satisfaction metrics
- Earnings
- Employee morale
- Quality
- Market Share

Why Companies Use a Balanced Scorecard

It is important to have balanced scorecards because it determines clear linkages between the strategies and the organization. Balance scorecards can help your company in many ways.

Some of these ways are listed below.

- It is used to simplify and update the strategy of a business. It is important to have a clear strategy so everyone concerned can have a hold of it to make it effective. There can be a sudden change in the strategy initially adopted by the company due to any reason, so a new strategy can be updated here for everyone to have a clear understanding.
- Make a linkage between strategic goals to annual budgets and long-term objectives. A connection

between objectives, annual budgets and long-term objectives can help increase the business's efficiency keeping all the resources in mind.

- Track the key elements of the business strategy. After a business strategy has been formed, it is important to keep a track of all the elements of the business strategy so that you know where you stand. Tracking and recording can help you in improving and moving towards growth and success.

- Incorporate strategic objectives into resource allocation processes. Strategies are implemented when the resources are allocated sensibly towards them. Objectives are achieved when the resource allocation is done rightly.

- Facilitate organizational change. Organizational change is inevitable, and change brings better opportunities. So, the scorecard helps in the facilitation of this adjustment.

- Do a comparison between the geographically diverse performance of different business units. Comparing the performance of diverse business units can help in many ways. If a performance of a specific unit is not good, then a root-cause analysis can be performed. The ability to expand can also be determined through this performance comparison.

- Enhance organization-wide comprehension of the corporate strategy and goals. The vision, mission, as well as strategy to achieve these things are spread widely in the company with the help of a balanced scorecard. Every employee has a better understanding and is motivated to increase efficiency.

What Should Managers Do to Design and Execute a Fair Scorecard?

- Articulating the strategy and goals of the business. Expressing your plan and strategy to the members of your business is essential because it gives a clear sense of direction to everyone. The employees will keep the vision in their minds and implement the strategy before removing forward with the process.
- Identifying the effectiveness metrics that most effectively connect the strategy and goal of the business to its outcomes. Effectiveness categories can include financial performance, operations, innovation, employee performance, etc. which can help us identify your position in the entire process.
- Establishing objectives that support the business vision and strategy. Once you have your mission and strategy with you, you need to set goals and objectives that will help you get what you have envisioned.
- Implementing effective metrics and relevant criteria, as well as setting both intermediate and final objectives. Here you set the duration and types of goals and targets you have. The measures that you will be taking to achieve your mission and goals.
- Ensuring company-wide acceptance of the measures. All the members of the company that are directly linked with these objectives need to have prior information about the measures that are designed to achieve your goals. Telling them about your

measures can help you gather better insight and further give everyone a direction.

- Creating appropriate budgeting, tracking, communication, and reward systems. These systems play a vital role in their operation process. They help you keep a track of budgeting, communications, and all other operations that need to be taken care of.
- Collecting and analyzing performance data and comparing actual results with desired performance. You already have performance categories in which you have desired or expected results. Once you have gotten hold of the data then you can compare it and find where you need improvement or how well you are doing.
- Take action to close unfavorable gaps. Once all the analysis has been conducted, that is when you can notice the gaps and problems that need special attention. Since you have all the data now, you can fill these gaps by taking suitable actions.

Standardizing

Standardizing is the process of evaluating the parameters of your firm to those of your industry rivals or innovative companies outside of your sector.

Common standardizing measures include:

- Profits
- Manufacturing expenses
- Labor attrition
- Production cycle duration

- Customer feedback

How Standardizing Works

- Pick a procedure, product, or service to standardize. This can be the product you want to improve or check the problems that might be occurring and causing fewer sales or issues.
- Identify the key performance metrics. These metrics can be financial, customer-focused, or process-focused. This will give an idea of all the features of a product and how they are doing against the set targets.
- Choose companies or internal areas to benchmark. Find the best and most competitive companies or internal areas to benchmark which have things in common with you. The most competitive can help you identify issues and improve.
- Collect data on performance and practices. The relevant data of the companies that you have chosen will be used for benchmarking.
- Examine the information and discover improvement opportunities. Once you have the data, you can check where your product is lagging, and which features can be improved to increase productivity and efficiency.
- Modify and apply the best practices while establishing acceptable objectives and obtaining company-wide adoption. This analysis will have you set more goals for the future to achieve your targets and improve.

Why Organizations Use Standardizing

- To enhance efficiency. The standardizing process identifies ways to enhance operational efficiency and product design. This increases the effectiveness and efficiency of the entire company as they improve themselves by comparing and finding room for betterment.

- To comprehend the relative position of costs. Standardizing highlights the relative cost position of a company and indicates areas for development. Once you understand your relative cost position, you increase business sales performance. This can increase the overall revenue of the business by increasing sales.

- To acquire strategic benefits. Standardizing assists businesses in concentrating on qualities that are essential for establishing strategic benefits. This gives your company a chance to be more successful than others. This allows you to outperform your competitors.

- To boost organizational learning rates. Standardizing Benchmarking introduces new concepts to the organization and enables the exchange of knowledge. This can help you bring more innovation and creativity to your business.

- To motivate employees. Frequent benchmarking provides an opportunity for the employees to increase their overall contribution to the company by being motivated. You can compare the productivity of employees in your business with employees of other companies and find room for improvement.

- To understand competition in a better way. Once you have analyzed your competitors, you have better data and information regarding them. You are aware of their process, methods of operations, and strategies. This also gives you a better competitor analysis.

Standardizing holds great importance in the business, as mentioned earlier in this section. At one time or another, every company needs to go through the process of benchmarking to improve the overall productivity of the company and stay in the competition.

Transformation

Taking a 'better, faster, and cheaper' approach.

Structured activities can increase efficiency, transparency, accountability, implementation, and the speed of decision-making. When you have everything lined up and have a proper structure, then it's easier to work in harmony and increase overall productivity.

- Differentiation Improvement

A performance-based action that encompasses business model, service, and product. This is a kind of strategy that helps the business provide something new and unique to the customers.

- Portfolio-related Moves

Active resource allocation, redistributing over 60% of its capital expenditures across its company or marketplace over a ten-year period. These actions generate 50% more worth than their equivalents.

Rethinking Your Strategy

There can be any reason that you might think of changing your strategy. If you have been experiencing frequent declines in your revenues or your promotion techniques are not targeting your consumers. These can be some solid reasons for rethinking your strategy.

Reasons to Change Your Strategies.

- Competitors

Competitors can play a huge role in changing your whole perspective towards business. If your competitors are evolving and they are filling the gaps, and this can help them move forward in the competition, this is a solid reason for you to change your strategy and remain ahead in the competition.

- Technology

Advancement in technology can change the costs, production time and development of the product or service you are offering. Moreover, technology change in the outside world can also restructure consumer behavior. This is where a business will change its strategy to manage the operational changes within the company and changes in the consumer market.

- Inconsistent Revenues

There can be any error that might result in declining or inconsistent revenue. There's a possibility that your departments are not performing well. Moreover, your promotional techniques can be outdated or not targeting the right audience. Such situations can be really concerning so this is where you start thinking about new strategies or some modifications to the existing ones.

- Regulations

Keeping the regulatory environment is not in your hands. Regulations and policies can be changed or altered at any time. These regulations can change the entire pattern of the industry in no time. You can easily lose your competitive advantage because of changes in regulations. So, with changing regulations you might want to rethink your business strategies.

These are some of the major reasons why your business or any other business needs to change and rethink its business strategies. The business environment is ever evolving in this modern era so change is really important, and it needs to happen.

Steps Towards Revamping Your Strategies

Does your strategy embrace those long odds and the uncertainty they imply? If not, revisit the way you devise a strategy.

- Roll With It

Ditch the annual for a rolling planning process that checks assumptions, revisits context and refreshes strategy. This is a kind of reality check and planning is done on a continual basis. This is not a rigid or strict processing technique. With changing behaviors of the industry and market, strategies also change.

- Make Choices

Force discussion about the combination of moves and scenarios with different levels of resources and risk. You need to make some tough decisions and make some choices looking at the current situation of your business. You need to look at all the possibilities and concerns of certain situations and then plan your strategy.

- Dig Deeper

To shift resources to the best opportunities, develop a detailed curve of 50 or so, specific, investable opportunities one level down from the business unit. You can't make decisions without enough information. You need to dig deeper and collect all the knowledge you require in refreshing your strategy and make it competitive.

- Go Baseless

Discard 'base case' assumptions that veil unrealistic aspirations. Instead, presume the business's current performance will continue; then find the strategic moves needed to alter that trajectory. Don't rely on assumptions as they can disrupt your future standing. Just examine and analyze your current situation.

- Take the First Step

Test the plan by breaking your strategy into six-month increments. If the first step isn't doable, the rest of the plan is bunkum. It is always better to take a test run first because this can give you a clearer idea if this strategy is going to be successful or not and is it even worth changing.

Every business has its own ways of strategizing and making changes. These are some generic steps that might help you get started with the entire process. Changes can be hard, not just for the leaders but for the entire team. This is where the managers and leaders weigh in by structuring the working culture in a way that everyone can adapt to new strategies and give their 100%.

End of Module Questions